Sleepwalking

Hannah Khalil

methuen | drama

LONDON • NEW YORK • OXFORD • NEW DELHI • SYDNEY

METHUEN DRAMA
Bloomsbury Publishing Plc
50 Bedford Square, London, WC1B 3DP, UK
1385 Broadway, New York, NY 10018, USA
29 Earlsfort Terrace, Dublin 2, Ireland

BLOOMSBURY, METHUEN DRAMA and the Methuen Drama logo are trademarks of
Bloomsbury Publishing Plc

First published in Great Britain 2021

Cover design by Tjaša Krivec

A catalogue record for this book is available from the British Library.

A cataog record for this book is available from the Library of Congress.

ISBN: PB: 978-1-3501-7728-4
       ePDF: 978-1-3501-7729-1
       eBook: 978-1-3501-7730-7

Series: Modern Plays

Typeset by RefineCatch Limited, Bungay, Suffolk
Printed and bound in Great Britain

To find out more about our authors and books visit www.bloomsbury.com
and sign up for our newsletters.

Author's note on Sleepwalking

Hannah Khalil February 2021

When I'm asked what advice I might give to writers just starting out I often say: "write your play as if it is never going to be produced." This might sound counter-productive, but if the subject matter is very close to you, or might be perceived as controversial, it is useful to be able to distance yourself from the worry of how it will be received and allow the piece to be unencumbered with any self-censorship. I certainly had to tell myself that when I was writing *Sleepwalking*, because the two Grannies in my life, who have enabled the writing of this and all of my other plays through their hands-on support with my daughter, are nothing like the Mother in *Sleepwalking*.

Once you have written your play you then have to do a volte face and believe with all your might that it will be produced. Because a play is never fully realised until it is breathed into three-dimensional life by a team of actors and creatives. And the struggle to get new plays on stage is a reality for every playwright I've ever met. So when you have that elusive 'yes' meeting with a theatre or producer or director, and they confirm that they will be mounting your play the elation is intoxicating. Production, of course, is another mountain to climb but to be given the guy ropes, climbing gear and supplies and sent on your way is joyous. I have many plays in drawers that have not been produced. But I have never been in the position of getting to base camp with a 'yes' and then having my expedition cancelled because of bad weather. Or a virus.

Of course, this is what happened with *Sleepwalking* which was programmed to open at Hampstead Theatre Downstairs in March 2020. What's even more heartbreaking is that we were just a few days from tech – when director Audrey Sheffield, actors Eileen Nicholas and Jeany Spark and the whole creative team would get into the theatre for the first time and prepare all the technical elements for the imminent production. But it was not to be. One minute we were in rehearsal, the next in lockdown and we never got to say goodbye. It's felt very strange, a sort of limbo of not knowing what will happen, not just with *Sleepwalking* but with our theatres and our industry. So, I am very grateful to Methuen for suggesting the publication of *Sleepwalking* as part of this series of Lost Plays. I hope you will enjoy reading it and that it will be 'found' in a theatre, as well as on a bookshelf, soon.

Sleepwalking was due to premiere at Hampstead Theatre Downstairs on 26 March 2020.

Cast

Mother　　Eileen Nicholas
Daughter　Jeany Spark

Writer Hannah Khalil
Director Audrey Sheffield
Designer Anna Reid
Lighting Ali Hunter
Sound Julian Starr

Sleepwalking

With gratitude and love
to all the Margarets in my life

Characters

Mother
Daughter

A Note on Design

The set, which is the interior of a suburban kitchen, should be as realistic as is possible within budgetary constraints. And, if feasible, as the play progresses it should gradually get dismantled piece by piece, so by the end there are only a few vital items on stage and perhaps the skeleton of the house.

Scene One

The kitchen of a suburban house. Evening. An older woman, the **Mother***, is wiping down the kitchen table, tidying after a child's meal.*

Pause.

A younger woman, the **Daughter***, enters through the back door.*

Daughter   Hello! Oh – let me do that.

Mother   It's fine.

Daughter   You don't need to clear up.

Mother   It's part of the job.

Daughter   It's not. It's really not.

A beat.

Mother   How was your day? You look tired.

Daughter   Fine. Busy. But at least I got away on time. Really, don't do that.

Mother   Would you like a cuppa? Sit down.

The **Daughter** *doesn't.*

Daughter   No – I'll make you one.

Mother   Just had one.

Daughter   You go and play with her.

Mother   She's fine.

Daughter   Pick-up ok?

Mother   No trouble. She's no trouble. But was ravenous. Four fish fingers she ate.

Daughter   Four?

Mother   Didn't like the lunch she said. Curry. Who serves children curry?

Daughter (*sotto voce*)   Indians?

Mother   Sorry?

Daughter   It's great she had a big tea anyway.

Mother   Have you thought about a packed lunch?

Daughter   Yes. But I like her to have a hot meal, especially in winter.

Mother   Mm.

Daughter   And she usually loves Mary's cooking. This is a one-off.

Mother   I'd make it – I know the sandwiches she likes.

Daughter   You're so sweet, but really it's ok.

Mother   I'd like to. Could do it the night before and leave it in the fridge all ready. Save you. You've enough to do.

Daughter   That's lovely. But I /

Mother   And with her allergies. Might be a safer option . . . Just think about it.

Daughter   Maybe in the summer. When it's warmer.

Mother   The offer's there.

A beat.

Daughter   Is she watching telly?

Mother   I got her a magazine, she's reading it in her room.

Daughter   Reading?

Mother   Well – you know colouring the pictures doing the little activities.

Daughter   Why don't you go and help her – I'll finish clearing up here.

Mother   It's done now.

Daughter   Thanks.

Mother   Am I on duty tomorrow?

Daughter   On –?

Mother   Do you need me?

Daughter   Oh. Thank you – no I'll do pick-up tomorrow.

Mother   Ok. Why don't you sit down. Rest. I can do her bedtime for you.

Daughter   It's ok.

Mother   You must be tired.

Daughter   Yes.

Mother   Well then?

Daughter   I want to see her.

A beat.

Mother   I understand. It does make the rest of the world go away doesn't it?

Daughter   Hm?

Mother   Being with her. You sort of focus in on her and nothing else matters. Know what I mean?

We hear a child's voice shouting 'MUMMY!' The **Mother** *jumps up and heads for the door to go to her.*

Daughter   I'll go.

Mother   Is she alright?

Daughter   Probably just done a poo.

Mother   If you want me to go to her I will.

Daughter   No it's fine. She's calling me. I'll go.

She goes.

The **Mother** *picks up the* **Daughter***'s coat that has been left on a chair and hangs it on the hook. She then goes to the kitchen door* *and opens it a crack, cocking her ear to hear the conversation happening between the child and the* **Daughter** *upstairs. She smiles approvingly at the happy sounds of chatting and laughing.*

Scene Two

The kitchen of a suburban house. Evening. An older woman, the **Mother***, sits at the kitchen table with a mug of tea. She is looking at the crossword.*

Pause.

A younger woman, the **Daughter***, enters through the back door. She moves slowly and quietly, gingerly taking the keys out of the door trying not to make a sound. When she turns around and sees the* **Mother** *at the table she jumps.*

Daughter   Oh it's you.

Mother   Who were you expecting?

Daughter   You scared me!

Mother   Evidently. How was work?

Daughter   I don't know why they leave everything till 6 o'clock. It's like they spend all bloody day drinking tea and then they realise – oh it's nearly time for her to go home, we better send her something to do.

Mother   Don't they have homes to go to?

Daughter   They're all about twelve, and it's like a competition to see who can stay the latest. Sorry.

Mother   Oh dear. Don't worry – I'm here.

Daughter   I thought you'd be watching telly.

Mother   I've gone off *Enders*. Since all that stabbing business.

Daughter   Right. Did you eat?

Mother   I'm not really hungry.

Daughter   But I told you – I left smoked salmon there – and potatoes. If I'd known I was going to be late I'd have plated it for you.

Mother   No need. It's fine.

Daughter   Thank you – so much – I'm sorry.

Mother   It's not your fault. Work.

Daughter   Do you want anything now – I'm going to heat some soup.

Mother   No. Thanks. Anyway she was no trouble.

Daughter   Good. Was she surprised when you turned up to get her?

Mother   No. Not really. Showed me her pictures on the walls. Then we came back. Have you seen her spaghetti one?

Daughter   Spaghetti?

Mother   It's this picture made from spaghetti and glitter and glue I suppose. Hers is rather good.

Daughter   I've not seen it.

Mother   Have you not? It's on the wall – as you walk in.

Daughter   I'll look tomorrow. Oh now where's the ladle. Bloody cleaner.

Mother   I thought you liked this one.

Daughter   She moves everything. And sometimes she throws things away.

Mother   What sort of things?

Daughter   I don't know, things – pots.

Mother   Cooking pots?

Daughter   No – plastic ones – from soup – I like to reuse them. But she bins them.

Mother   You should tell her.

Daughter   She doesn't speak English.

Mother   How does she know what to do?

Daughter   I text her boss, who then texts her in Bulgarian.

Mother   Funny arrangement.

Daughter   And look at the tea towels. Why does she put them like that? I bet she's put all the clothes from my chair in the wash basket. She always does that – who asks her to? She's not even done the washing-up today. Fiddling with the tea towels but leaves a full sink.

Mother   Shall I go and check on her?

Daughter   Why?

Mother   Just make sure.

Daughter   How long ago did she fall asleep?

Mother   An hour?

Daughter   That's late – was she upset?

Mother   No. I just don't like to rush her. She had a good play in the bath. Shall I check her?

Daughter   No. She'll be fine. I'll go in a sec.

A beat.

Oh. The cleaner didn't take her money.

Mother   No.

Daughter   Why didn't she take her money?

Mother   I don't think she's been.

Daughter   They never text to say . . . then who – the tea towels.

Mother   I did that.

Daughter   You didn't say, you let me go on and on and you didn't say.

Mother   Well. I might go and check her.

Daughter   Why?

Mother   Only – she woke up not long ago.

Daughter   Did she?

Mother   Yes. Crying.

Daughter   Oh.

Mother   A bad dream I think.

Daughter   Did she say anything?

Mother   I couldn't really make it out. She was crying.

Daughter   Oh.

Mother   You know sometimes I find it hard to understand what she says. You kind of have to tune your ear into her little phrases and things. Do you find that?

Daughter   No. But this dream – was she very distressed?

Mother   As distressed as I've seen her. She was calling for you.

Daughter   Oh no – was she? And I wasn't here.

Mother   Don't worry. I told her you'd be back soon. That you'd be back and go and stroke her.

Daughter   I feel dreadful now. Bloody work.

Mother   You couldn't help it. Why don't you . . . [go up].

Daughter   They're all so young. No commitments.

Mother   Not so long ago that was you.

Daughter   Seems like for ever. Maybe I'll take her into bed with me tonight.

Mother   Don't start that. She'll never want to go in her own room again.

A beat.

Would you like me to stay? I could go in the spare room – if she wakes up I'll sort her out, save you getting disturbed. You've work tomorrow. You're tired.

Daughter   You're very kind. But no. No. That's fine. You saved me today – but go on, go home. I'll be ok – we'll be ok my girl and me. She won't have any more bad dreams now I'm home.

Scene Two – Night

The kitchen. It is the middle of the night. Dark. The phone starts to ring. It is a hard sound in the dark. It rings and rings.

Then it stops as suddenly as it started.

Scene Three

The kitchen of the suburban house. Evening. The **Mother** *is washing up.*

Pause.

A younger woman, the **Daughter**, *enters through the back door. Again she moves slowly and quietly, gingerly taking the keys out of the door trying not to make a sound until she spots the* **Mother** *washing up.*

Daughter   Don't tell me she didn't come again today.

Mother   She came. She just didn't wash up properly. I picked up a cup for her milk and it had bits in it.

Daughter   Useless.

Mother   You look tired.

Daughter   I am.

Mother   You're later than I thought.

Daughter   I know – sorry I had a meeting that ran over and over –

Mother   Never mind. You're home now. Early night.

Daughter   Yes. Was she ok?

Mother   Yes – but – now don't get worried but – she hurt herself today.

Daughter   What? How? Nobody called me.

Mother   Nothing serious.

Daughter   They're meant to call me if something happens – what happened?

Mother   She just caught her finger in the door.

Daughter   She didn't – oh that's painful.

Mother   There's hardly any bruise – they put ice on it and everything. I had to sign the accidents book when I collected her.

Daughter   They have an accidents book?

Mother   Of course. Health and safety.

Daughter   I just never thought about it. She's not very accident prone is she?

Mother   I suppose she's not no. Dangerous though. Thinking that.

Daughter   Why is it dangerous?

Mother   You know – now you've said that she's bound to have an accident. My mother always said never tempt fate – asking for trouble.

Daughter   What do you mean?

Mother   Sod's law isn't it? You say she's not accident prone she has an accident.

Daughter   It's not my fault! I wasn't even there.

A beat.

No. She had one today. That's her accident. Done.

A beat.

Mother   I might just go and check on her.

Daughter   She'll be fine. Don't fuss.

A beat.

What? Did something *else* happen?

Mother   Well, I don't want to worry you, but when she was in the bath I noticed something – a rash.

Daughter   A rash? Where?

Mother   On her back.

Daughter   What kind of rash?

Mother   I wondered about her allergies.

Daughter   You didn't give her eggs?

Mother   No – course not –

Daughter   What did it look like? Did you take a photo of it?

Mother   I didn't think to do that. I was in a bit of a flap.

Daughter   It was bad then. What was it like?

Mother   Sort of white spots – raised a bit.

Daughter   Oh no.

Mother   And they itched her like mad. She was wailing.

Daughter   Why didn't you call me?

Mother   I panicked a bit to be honest with you. I've not seen a rash like that. But then I pulled myself together and thought, well, I've raised two children I can deal with this. And then I remembered your emergency sheet.

*She indicates the back of the kitchen door where the **Daughter** has printed out a list of emergency information for her child.*

Mother   But of course she's in the bath. Wailing. And you know they say never leave a child in the bath alone. Not for a second. But then I thought she always does. She always leaves her in the bath for a minute, just to go and get some water or the themometer. She always does it. /

Daughter   / Not always . . . /

Mother   / So I dashed down and read the instructions. I knew she wasn't drowning because I could hear her crying. And there I saw what stuff you've got for allergies. So I gave her a dose.

Daughter   How much?

Mother   Don't worry I checked. And it was magic. Worked like magic. Rash gone in minutes, tears gone, out the bath and she was asleep before the end of the first story. /

Daughter   / Crying tired her out.

Mother   / Crying tired her out. That's what I thought – poor love.

Pause.

Daughter   What gave her that rash. I wonder. Did you give her a snack before bed?

Mother   Nothing unusual.

Daughter   I'll have to ask them what the menu was yesterday for her.

Mother   May be time to think about a packed lunch . . .

Daughter   Maybe. Did she say anything before it came up?

Mother   No – she was happily playing in the bath – playing . . . a game.

Daughter   What game? Why did you stop?

Mother   Just a game.

Daughter   Tell me – or I'll worry.

Mother   Well – it was just – mummys and babies. She said her baby was crying – was missing its mummy . . . but that was just the game.

Daughter   Right.

A beat.

The rash must be something she ate.

Mother   I should go and check on her.

Daughter   No don't – leave her the poor thing – let her sleep a bit more. She's tired . . .

A beat.

I might have a glass of wine. Do you want one?

Mother   No. I never drink when I'm on duty.

Daughter   But –

Mother   I better be off. Unless you want me to stay?

Daughter   No – that's ok. Sorry about all the drama.

Mother   No trouble. She's no trouble at all.

The **Mother** *begins to put on her coat, hat and gloves, and the* **Daughter** *pours herself a glass of wine.*

Mother   By the way – she told me she's been sleeping with you in your bed. She asked if she could go in there at bedtime.

Daughter   What did you say?

Mother   I told her no.

A beat.

You've not been doing that have you?

Daughter   Only sometimes.

Mother   I warned you about that. My sister did that with hers. Husband ended up on the sofa. For years. Poor man.

Daughter   It's just easier than getting up to her in the night.

Mother   Does she wake every night?

Daughter   Not every night.

Mother   Misses him I suppose.

Daughter   I suppose.

Scene Three – Night

The kitchen. It is the middle of the night. Dark. The phone starts to ring.

Daughter *enters in her night clothes. She is very sleepy. She stands in the doorway staring at the phone. Perhaps she puts a hand on it, considering. Before she can decide whether to answer it, it stops. She keeps staring at it. Did she dream it ringing?*

Scene Four

The kitchen. Evening. The **Mother** *is loading the washing machine with sheets.*

The **Daughter** *enters through the back door, quietly as ever, but more normally when she spots the* **Mother**.

Daughter   Why are you doing that?

Mother   Hello. I thought I'd save you the trouble.

Daughter   I wish you wouldn't. You're here for her. That's enough.

Mother   It's fine.

Daughter   It's nothing that can't wait.

Mother   Thanks for the quiche. It was delicious. Did you make it?

Daughter   I got it in the new deli.

Mother   By the station? It was lovely. I left you a piece to try.

Daughter   I don't like quiche. Take it home with you. Do you want tea?

Mother   No. Thanks. You look tired. Another bad day at work you poor thing?

Daughter   No it was the night . . . I was – disturbed.

Mother   What by?

Daughter   Mainly her. She's awful to share a bed with. Starts in a normal position but after an hour or two manoeuvres herself around so she's horizontal and last night she rested her feet on my throat. I'm not joking. At points I could barely breath.

Mother   Why didn't you move her?

Daughter   It seemed cruel to wake her.

Mother   How did you manage to sleep?

Daughter   I didn't – really. So today at work I was so tired. At one point I started nodding off in the middle of an email, I was actually typing asleep – sleep typing – so I did something I've never done before. I went to the front desk and asked for the key to the sick room. The man asked what was wrong – that he'd need to report it to my manager but I couldn't have her knowing – she's looking for an excuse to get rid of me, so you know what I said – I lied and said I was breastfeeding and needed to express milk. He looked shocked – a bit disgusted – or maybe scared – I'm not sure which and gave me the key and I went and locked the door of the sick room – lay down on the bed, set my alarm and slept for half an hour. It was absolute bliss. But then I spent the rest of the afternoon paranoid someone would know – would figure it out, that I'd been literally sleeping on the job.

Mother   How would they?

Daughter   Maybe a line on my face from the pillow – or someone saw me going in – or – I don't know.

Mother   It was your lunch break wasn't it?

Daughter   Yes but no one takes lunch breaks. They sit at their desk with a sandwich or a pot of something and eat and type at the same time. It's pretty disgusting when you think about it. It's like there's someone monitoring how many hours they are at their desk and rewarding or punishing them accordingly. I suppose there is – she's always watching. That's why I got nervous she'd notice. I told them I was in a brainstorm session. Why are you washing sheets?

Mother   Oh. Well. She had an accident.

Daughter   What? When?

Mother   Not long ago . . .

Daughter   After she'd gone to bed?

Mother   Yes.

Daughter   When she was asleep?

Mother   Yes.

Daughter   What happened?

Mother   She was fine when I picked her up – she always is nowadays – expects it I suppose. And she had a snack and then her bath, we did two stories – she wanted three, but I said that no Granny had to have her dinner. And then I held her hand a bit until she went off. Then I came downstairs for my quiche – which was lovely. And when I'd finished I thought I'll go and check she's ok, and she was ok – she was asleep – but she'd kicked off the covers and as I put my hand down to pull them up I felt it was wet and for a minute I thought she was sweating – lord I thought what a lot of sweat and then it dawned on me that it wasn't sweat at all. And I thought it's still early – I can't leave her like this all night – so I carried her into your bed and changed her clothes, then I changed her bed and put her back. And she never woke up. At all.

A beat.

You didn't tell me she was still doing that. I thought all that was done with months ago.

Daughter   It was. It's been . . . ages. Did you put her on the toilet before bath?

Mother   Of course. I always follow your instructions to the letter.

Daughter   Well, I don't know what to say. It's very odd.

Mother   Don't worry about it. It's nothing. A little regression. Happens to them all one way or another.

Daughter   It never happens when I'm here.

A beat.

Mother   Well. She'll be fine. I do think you should stop having her in your bed though. That can't help. And you aren't sleeping. Sleep is so important.

Daughter   Well, maybe tonight will be the last night.

Mother   Why? Just stop now.

Daughter   I promised her this morning that when I got in I'd bring her into bed with me.

Mother   She won't remember.

Daughter   She will. She remembers everything. And besides. I want to remember – the last night that she slept with me.

Mother   What do you mean?

Daughter   Do you remember the last time that you held him? The last time you changed his nappy? The last time you fed him or cleaned his face? They just go these things and I want to try and remember them all.

Mother   They go to be replaced by other things. I didn't think you were so soft.

A beat.

I mean that you take things so to heart . . . Well – I'll bring that bit of quiche home with me then.

Daughter   Do.

Mother   Unless you want it?

Daughter   No. Thanks. I don't like it.

A beat.

Mother   Are you sure you don't want me to stay?

Scene Four – Night

The kitchen. It is the middle of the night. Dark. **Daughter** *enters in her night clothes. She is very sleepy. She approaches the phone, picks it up and listens – there is no one there.*

She replaces it. She turns to go back upstairs then has an idea. She goes back to the phone, takes it off the hook and leaves it off the hook. Satisfied, she goes back upstairs to bed.

Scene Five

The kitchen, evening. It is empty. There is a pile of little girl's clothes on the table.

The **Daughter***'s key is in the door, cautious as ever. When she enters she is surprised that the* **Mother** *is not there. She puts down her bag, takes off her coat. She moves around the kitchen – messes up the tea towels which the* **Mother** *has arranged again. She nods to herself and goes upstairs.*

Pause.

The **Daughter** *re-enters. She seems exasperated. She goes to her handbag and takes out a packet of cigarettes. She thinks for a moment then replaces them. Instead she goes to the fridge and takes out a bottle of wine. Pours a glass. Downs it. Pours another.*

The **Mother** *enters. She has clearly been asleep.*

She's still half asleep. Yawning a little.

Mother   Sorry.

Daughter   Don't be. You're tired. She can be exhausting.

Mother   No, no it's not her – she's no trouble. It was just – dark and –

Daughter   Why are these clothes here?

Mother   I noticed all these things had holes in them – nothing major – but little nicks – here and there – if left they'll grow into great big gaping things so I was going to take them home and darn them for her.

Daughter   You don't need to do that.

Mother   I'd like to. Now she's at nursery every day it gives me something to do . . . She doesn't need to be there every day you know, I love having her.

Daughter   We have talked about this, she does need to be there every day, it's the way that place works. It's all or nothing. Besides. It's good for her – get her ready for school.

Mother   She's so little though.

A beat.

Did you notice I took off her clothes?

Daughter   What?

Mother   She was so hot.

Daughter   Did she have a temperature?

Mother   I think so.

Daughter   You think so? Did you check?

Mother   I don't know how to use that high-tech thermometer. My mother used to know me so well – know my body so well she could just look at me and know if I was ill. I was the same. Intuitive.

Daughter   She was hot?

Mother   Very, but she was asleep so I stripped her off. That's why I stayed up there to keep an eye on her.

Daughter   Ok.

Mother   She had a good tea. Fish fingers. Ate them all. Never mind the disturbances.

Daughter   Disturbances?

Mother   Phone never stopped ringing.

Daughter   Really – who was it?

Mother   First one was a crackly line. Man's voice – hard to make out . . . for a second I thought . . . then he said he was Arthur from Foxtons . . .

Daughter   Did he leave a number?

Mother   No, said he would try your mobile.

Daughter   Great.

Mother   Foxtons – sounds like a solicitors?

Daughter   No – it's the new gym I'm considering joining.

Mother   Oh. Good idea.

Daughter   Good idea?

Mother   Keep fit. Important. Once you've had a child. Your body shape changes doesn't it? I'm not being – mine did – everyone's does. Part of becoming a mum. Stomach's never the same again after –

Daughter   And boobs after breastfeeding.

Mother   That's all I meant. Health wise . . . it's important. I wasn't saying anything.

Daughter   I know. (*She swigs from the wine glass.*)

Mother   And they won't approve of that you know – at Foxtons gym. (*Indicating the wine glass the* **Daughter** *is nursing.*)

Daughter   Who else called? (**Mother** *looks confused.*) You said disturban*ces*.

Mother   Oh. Yes. It was that woman from the cleaning company. To say your usual one is going back to Bulgaria – something about her visa – but that she has someone new ready for you.

Daughter   Oh I liked that one – What? I did. She wasn't perfect but she used to do this nice thing with the loo roll, fold it into a little arrow at the end. Like in hotels . . . What a pain.

Mother   That's what I said.

Daughter   Having to train someone new up – show her how I like things.

Mother   That's what I said.

Daughter   I just don't have the time or the energy.

Mother   That's why I cancelled them!

Daughter   Cancelled?

Mother   I told them not to bother, that you'd make other arrangements.

Daughter   Why would you do that?

Mother   You always complain about them. I thought you'd be pleased . . .

Daughter   I need a cleaner!

Mother   I know.

Daughter   I have a job –

Mother   I know –

Daughter   I can't spend the few precious hours I have here scrubbing –

Mother   I'm going to do it.

Daughter   You're – what?

Mother   I clean my own house. Always have. And since she's at nursery I've lots of free time.

Daughter   Then take up bingo – or go swimming!

Mother   Bingo?

Daughter   I am not comfortable with you cleaning my house.

Mother   It would save you a lot of money. Things must be hard now you have to pay for this place alone . . . and I'd like to, then I could make sure her room is spotless – I never trusted that one . . .

Daughter   It's very kind, but it is absolutely out of the question. I couldn't have you cleaning up after us. You do so much already. Too much.

Mother   I don't –

Daughter   I'll call them tomorrow and sort it out.

Mother   Ok. I didn't mean to offend you – I thought I was doing a nice thing.

Daughter   I'm not offended. It's a really nice thought but it's not on.

Mother   Right. Well, I better get home.

Daughter   Do you want to stay and eat with me?

Mother   No – I feel tired, I'll get home.

She puts her hat and coat on.

Want me to check on her before I go?

Daughter   No. That's fine. I'll go now, make sure she's not cold.

A beat.

Can I ask you something though – why did you sleep in my bed?

Mother   What?

Daughter   You said you dropped off while keeping an eye on her, so how come you were in my room not hers?

Mother   Was I?

Daughter   Yes. You were sleeping in my bed.

Mother   Not on the chair in her room?

Daughter   No.

Mother   Are you sure?

Daughter   Quite sure.

Mother   Funny. I don't remember going into your room at all . . .

Scene Five – Night

We can hear the feet on the stairs climbing up and down. It is the **Daughter**. *We cannot see her but we can hear her.*

She cannot sleep. She is waiting for the phone to ring. But it doesn't. She enters the kitchen – she picks it up, listens, then puts it down. She goes to leave but it starts to ring – she stares at it horrified.

Scene Six

*The kitchen. Late. The **Mother** sits at the kitchen table. She is waiting.*

Pause.

*The **Daughter** enters through the back door. She is trying very hard to be quiet but she is tipsy. Seeing the **Mother** at the table she jumps.*

Daughter   What are you doing here?

Mother   It's late.

Daughter   It's not supposed to be you.

Mother   That girl had to get home.

Daughter   She's sixteen.

Mother   She's still at school. It's a school night. You were meant to be back by 10. It's gone 12.

Daughter   I know.

Mother   She tried to call you. But your phone's off.

Daughter   It ran out of juice.

Mother   So she called me – from the emergencies sheet – and I came.

Daughter   Oh.

A beat.

Thanks. Sorry. I better plug this in then.

She plugs the phone in to a charger that is in the wall.

Jesus – twelve messages.

Mother   She was worried. I was worried.

Daughter   They got on ok though?

Mother   I don't know. She's not woken up anyway.

Daughter   Good.

Mother   Work was it?

Daughter   Yes. We had a big event today. We've been building up to it for months. It went well. That's why . . .

Mother   I see. You could have asked me to babysit you know.

Daughter   I know – but I always do. It's not fair.

Mother   I don't mind. I like it.

Daughter   I know. But I need to have other people I can call if /

Mother   She's a child – I think it's too much responsibility for her.

Daughter   She's a teenager. Her parents are across the road – she's the oldest of four – she's a lovely girl.

Mother   I'm sure.

A beat.

But I don't think she put her cream on after the bath you know.

Daughter   Oh.

Mother   Her eczema will come back. And you should have seen the state of the kitchen.

Daughter   I'll tell her. For next time.

Mother   Next time? You can't intend to use her again?

Daughter   Why? She's asleep – happily – without incident.

Mother   We don't know that. We don't know what happened when we weren't with her. Do we? She's so precious. So little. Anything could happen.

Daughter   Yes, but she's ok isn't she? You've checked on her.

Mother   Of course.

Daughter   Well then.

A beat.

Mother   Have you been smoking?

Daughter   Sorry?

Mother   I can smell /

Daughter   I'm an adult. I can do what I like.

Mother   If you bring her to bed with you she'll get the fumes.

Daughter   I haven't been /

Mother   It's bad for her.

Daughter   She hasn't been in bed with me for some time.

Mother   Good. You are smoking then?

Daughter   No.

She goes to pour herself a glass of wine.

Mother   Wouldn't you rather tea? If you've work tomorrow – I'll make you one.

Daughter   No. Nope. Thanks – I want one more of these.

Mother *watches her.*

Daughter   I'm sorry I was late. And that you got the call. It won't happen again.

A beat.

I was letting off steam.

Mother   Just ask me. To help. It's what I'm here for. I want to.

Daughter   Thanks.

Mother   Shall I /

Daughter   Gosh – you should go – it's very late – do you want me to call you a cab?

Mother   No – no it's just ten minutes walk.

Daughter   If you're sure.

Mother   And I'll get her tomorrow as agreed.

Daughter   Actually – I meant to say – there's a change of plan –

Mother   What?

Daughter   I don't need you to get her tomorrow.

Mother   You're not sending that girl?

Daughter   No. I'm going.

Mother   Really? Will you be able to get away in time? You don't want her left waiting.

Daughter   It's fine.

Mother   She won't be happy if she's the last one to be collected.

Daughter   She won't be.

Mother   But you said they always send you work at the last minute –

Daughter   It's ok. I've taken a half-day. I'll be there.

Mother   Oh. Ok – good. Well, just make sure you warn her, because she'll be expecting me. She remembers everything.

Daughter   Of course I'll tell her.

Mother *puts on her hat, coat and gloves.*

Mother   Because she doesn't like change, and I don't want her upset.

Scene Six – Night

The kitchen. It is the middle of the night. Dark. We have to focus our eyes to see. And once we can we notice the **Daughter** *is in there – she is lying on the floor. Her eyes wide open. Is she asleep or awake?*

Suddenly she sits up and looks at the phone. At that moment it starts to ring.

The **Daughter** *just stares at it.*

Scene Seven

The kitchen. Early evening. The **Daughter** *moves around the kitchen. She is tidying.*

Pause.

The **Mother** *enters through the back door.*

Mother   Is she in bed already?

Daughter   Yes.

Mother   You're very quick. I hoped I'd see her.

Daughter   She was tired.

Mother   Yes. Did you have a nice time together?

Daughter   Yes.

Mother   What did you do?

Daughter   Baked some cakes.

Mother   Oh. That's nice.

Daughter   Then we went to the cafe and she did some craft – a picture of you.

Mother   Did she?

Daughter   Let me show you.

She goes to her bag and rummages. Her passport falls out onto the floor. The **Mother** *picks it up and looks at it before handing it back to the* **Daughter** *who has now found the drawing.*

Daughter   There. Isn't it great.

Mother   It is.

Daughter   The ears aren't right – she rushed it a bit at the end – she was keen to get to the park.

Mother   The park as well? She'll have been in her element . . . Which one?

Daughter   The one with the sand pit.

Mother   Did you remember the bucket and spade?

Daughter   I did – she reminded me.

Mother   Well. I never take her to that one because of the sand. I always worry we'll bring it into the house.

Daughter   Oh.

Mother   So it would've been a nice treat for her is what I'm getting at.

Daughter   Yes.

A beat.

Mother   She's had a lovely day. Done so much. Must be overtired. Did she get all screamy at bedtime?

Daughter   Yes. But I love that. The freeness of it. Not sitting quietly like girls are meant to but running around madly. Being loud and alive like she's holding on to the day – the last bits of being awake.

Mother   And then she flakes out. Exhausted.

Daughter   Yes.

A beat.

Did you want a cup of tea?

Mother   No. I just – I remembered I promised to bring her some of these biscuits. She likes these ones. I'll put them in the cupboard.

A beat.

Daughter   Thanks. She was talking about him a lot today.

Mother   He always took her to the sand pit. Such a lovely dad. That's why. That's another reason I don't . . .

Daughter   She asked me if we could have a funeral.

Mother   What? What have you been saying to her?

Daughter   Saying to her? Nothing – why do you think I'd /

Mother   How would a child leap to that conclusion?

Daughter   He's not here. Is he? What else should she think?

Mother   How does she even know what death is?

Daughter   Because people die –

Mother   Who – who dies?

Daughter   People – in her telly programmes, animals, things – die.

Mother   It still doesn't explain how she made that leap.

Daughter   She thinks. She's clever. Why would I tell her he's dead? Why would I do that?

Mother   I don't know.

A beat.

It's just strange.

Daughter   No. He was here. Now he isn't. And she is trying to understand it.

Pause.

Mother   Aren't we all.

Daughter   Anyway how do we know he's not dead?

Mother   He's not dead.

Daughter   We don't know that.

Mother   He's not dead.

Daughter   How could he leave . . . never mind me – her – how could he leave her?

Mother   He's not dead.

I'm his mother. A mother knows things – feels them. When her child isn't well. Isn't happy. I sat up with him nights. When he had fever, sweats, was delirious. I was the one there. His blood came from me. So if something had happened to him – something wrong, something bad, if he wasn't alive anymore I'd know it. I'd know it.

Pause.

What goes on inside a relationship is never clear to the people outside.

Daughter   You think he left because of me?

Mother   He had his reasons. But he will be back. When the time is right.

Daughter   I don't know how long I can go on like this. Here.

Mother   What do you mean?

Daughter   Well – it's not easy being in this house. And if he's not here do we need all this space? When she asked about a funeral today it got me thinking may be we should do something – closure . . . Have a service. /

Mother   / But he's not dead /

Daughter   And then she and I could . . .

Mother   Could what?

Daughter   I don't know – move may be.

Mother   Move? You can't move.

Daughter   I can't stay here indefinitely – we bought this house thinking we would both be paying for it. I can't keep it up on my own much longer . . .

Mother   I could help out. Move in.

Daughter   No no no. Thank you – but no. It's not necessary. We will manage – she and I. But I was thinking about going north. Nearer to my sister.

Mother   You can't. What about your job? Her nursery?

Daughter   There are jobs and nurseries everywhere.

Mother   What if he comes back?

Daughter   What if he doesn't? I don't know how long I'm supposed to wait. Wonder what's happened to him. Carry it all. Not knowing. Day after day.

Mother   But – I'm here.

Daughter   Exactly – you'll be here if he comes back won't you.

Mother   You can't move. She'd hate it. She loves this house – her room. She'd miss all that. I'd miss her.

Daughter   I know. Oh. Please don't worry – it's just an idea. I had it today. I'm not fixed on it. Not at all. It's just a thought . . .

Pause.

I've upset you . . . I didn't mean to upset you. I'm just talking. Ignore me.

Mother   Shall I go and check on her.

Daughter   If you like.

Mother   I think I heard her coughing there.

Daughter   Maybe – she's getting a cold.

Mother   Did she not wear her hat today?

A beat.

I'll bring up a bowl of hot water.

Daughter   Why?

Mother   I always do – the steam makes the air nicer for her.

Daughter   Ok.

Mother   Don't worry I put it up high on the window ledge so if she got up in the night she wouldn't hurt herself.

Daughter   She never gets up, just calls.

Mother   I know. But things change.

A beat.

He used to sleepwalk you know.

Daughter   Did he?

Mother   I found him in the garden one night, the bath another. One time he was going out the front door and I caught him just in time. In his pyjamas.

Daughter   What happened if you woke him up?

Mother   Oh I never did that. Can be dangerous they say to wake a sleepwalker. They'd have a shock. Might faint. Or get violent. Or even drop dead. No you have to handle them with care.

Daughter   How strange. When did he grow out of it?

Mother   I don't know. I don't know if he ever did.

Daughter   I don't think he ever sleepwalked in all the time we lived together.

Mother   You're a deep sleeper yourself aren't you – you wouldn't notice. But I noticed. My boy.

Daughter   I never knew that about him. Strange he hid that from me. There was a time there I thought we knew every little thing about each other. . .

*The **Mother** has been boiling the kettle and now pours the water into a bowl.*

Mother   I'll just take this up to her.

*She exits. The **Daughter** sighs.*

Scene Seven – Night

*The kitchen. It is the middle of the night. Dark. We have to focus our eyes to see. The phone rings – the **Daughter** is stood by it. She is desperate. She cannot bear the noise. She lifts the receiver and replaces it. The ringing continues.*

She hits the receiver on the wall several times. Still it rings.

She takes the phone to the sink. She holds it gingerly like it is burning her – like the noise is hurting her physically.

She fills the sink with water and holds the telephone over it. She intends to drop it into the water to stop it. But just as she is about to the ringing stops.

She throws the phone onto the floor.

Scene Eight

The kitchen. Evening. It is empty.

Pause.

The **Mother** *enters through the back door. She has a carrier bag. She places it on the table and takes out a ballet outfit – leotard, tutu, tights and ballet slippers. She leaves them on the table. She looks in the fridge. She goes out of the kitchen to look for the* **Daughter**.

A beat.

She returns to the kitchen in a hurry.

The **Daughter** *follows not far behind. She looks unkempt – perhaps doing up a button on her top.*

Daughter   I didn't know you were coming.

Mother   Evidently.

Daughter   You didn't knock.

Mother   I have a key.

Daughter   Why – why didn't you tell me you were coming?

Mother   I was at home and I saw that I still had her ballet kit and I thought, I'd better take that over – if I don't take that over she'll have to do ballet in the blue leotard and she'll be the only one and she'll hate that she'll really, really hate that. She hates being different.

Daughter   But you usually call.

Mother   I know. It was a whim. I'll call in future.

Pause.

The sound of the front door slamming.

Gone then.

A beat.

Daughter   Do you want a drink / I want a drink.

She gets a glass of wine.

Mother   No no – I'm not staying – just came to drop those in.

Pause.

Did she go down alright?

Daughter   Yes. Exhausted. They did a little trip to the library.

Mother   The library? They didn't walk?

Daughter   Yes.

Mother   Is that safe?

Daughter   They don't go alone. They have adults with them. And they wear little vests – luminous ones – you can't miss them.

Mother   Still . . .

Pause.

Shall I go and check on her.

Daughter   She's fine. Don't worry.

Mother   But /

Daughter   She's fine.

A beat.

Mother   Did she know you were having company this evening?

Daughter   No.

Mother   You didn't introduce them?

Daughter   No.

A beat.

Mother   Well, that's something. Is this a new thing – I mean should I expect –?

Daughter   Look I'm a human being. I need /

Mother   What?

Daughter   I'm not the same person I was before I had her.

Mother   Everyone puts on weight. That's why you're going to the gym.

Daughter   No it's not about my body shape. I know I'm fatter I don't care about that really . . . Well, I do but I can live with that. I know it was years ago but I still can't understand it – my sweat smells different, I smell different . . . My skin is dry – cracking – and my hair just sticks to my head, lifeless, exhausted, dead. My boobs are like bananas and they're hairy – no one told me they'd get hairy – I pluck them, with tweezers.

Mother   For goodness sake! All this talk – I don't understand you lot, what did you expect?

Daughter   Expect?

Mother   From motherhood – it's a job.

Daughter   I know that. I knew that. Just nobody told me . . . the important things – like that I'd feel horrid, sore, scratchy all the time – there. I showed the doctor, she said it was to be expected, it was fine, apparently most women deal with much worse.

Mother   Then why are you complaining?

Daughter   I'm just trying to explain that I feel – not me – not good – surely you can relate to that? So when someone shows an interest /

Mother   You jump at the chance.

Daughter   That's not fair.

Mother   And him not gone long.

Daughter   It's been long enough. I deserve /

Mother   You're a mother. First.

Daughter   Yes – but /

Mother   No buts. That was your choice. You are a mother.

Daughter   I know that.

The sound of crying from upstairs.

Mother   You see. She knew. She sensed something was wrong. She doesn't like change. She's intuitive. I'll go to her.

Daughter   But /

The **Mother** *has already gone.*

Scene Eight – Night

The kitchen. It is the middle of the night. Dark. We have to focus our eyes to see. The **Daughter** *is lying across the table asleep. Suddenly the phone rings – it has been ringing on and off all night – the* **Daughter** *is desperate. She piles the chairs up on the table into a precarious tower. She takes the phone and climbs to the top.*

She holds the phone over her head, she's crying – about to throw it from this great height and possibly herself. The phone stops. She throws it down and then the chairs in turn. She is making a lot of noise. Sobbing.

Suddenly we hear a little cry of 'MUMMY!' from upstairs. Everything freezes. The **Daughter** *is panicked. Blackout.*

Scene Nine

The kitchen. Empty. Early evening. The **Mother** *enters through the back door. She is surprised no one is there. She puts down a supermarket plastic bag on the table. She looks in the fridge.*

Pause.

She goes into the hall.

Pause.

We hear her feet on the stairs going up.

Pause.

We hear her feet on the stairs coming down, faster and more agitated.

She dashes into the kitchen and grabs the telephone. She stops to think who she should call.

She puts the phone down again.

She picks it up and holds in in her hand – she never dials a number or lifts the phone to her ear, she just grips it tight as if it is a weapon and speaks.

Mother   What have you done? HOW COULD YOU. . . HOW COULD YOU TAKE HER. Look – Look – Just come back. You can't – you can't do this. You can't take her away from her home, her friends, her family – me yes me – please just come back. Bring her home.

Don't mind about him – or about the past. Maybe you blame me – that he's gone. Everyone always blames the mother. I blame myself. No. No I don't I blame you. You were never kind enough to him. At the beginning you were all over each other. But once she came along everything changed – didn't it? And then you were cold with him. And he's a man. He needed – affection. Love. And you couldn't – you didn't . . . So no I don't think he's dead – I think he left – you – not her, not me but you because you are a selfish, cold person. And because you couldn't keep him happy he left you. And me and her.

But forget that – forget all of that. Just come back. I'll pretend nothing happened. You pretend nothing happened. We'll continue as normal. As we have been.

She's mine. My girl. I lost my boy because of you – I can't lose her too. Don't, don't, don't, don't, don't /

The sound of keys in the back door. The **Daughter** *comes in. She smiles and then notices the look on the* **Mother***'s face.*

The **Mother** *who is still holding the phone in her hand stares aghast.*

Daughter   / What's the matter?

The **Mother** *stares at her.*

Daughter   What? Who's on the phone?

The **Mother** *stares.*

Daughter   Is it him? It's him isn't it – give it to me.

Mother   NO – no it's /

The **Daughter** *has grabbed the phone.*

Daughter   Hello? Hello? Are you there – you you bastard – where are you – I don't care just – hello? Hello?

Mother   It's not him – it's not him.

Daughter   Hello?

Mother   It's not him. Give it to me.

She takes the phone and hangs up.

They are both shaken.

Daughter   What was that about? You looked . . .

Mother   I got a shock.

Daughter   Why – what happened?

Mother   I came to see you and no one was here and –

Daughter   What?

Mother   Well – I thought you had . . . gone.

Daughter   Gone – where?

Mother   After the conversation we had last week. And I saw the passport in your bag –

Daughter   ID – for the gym.

Mother   – then I come here. And it's empty.

Daughter   You thought? – I wouldn't do that! Just go, all our stuff's here.

Mother   One of her bags was gone – the butterfly one /

Daughter   But why would I run – we're not fugitives!

Mother   I know I know I just got a shock. Sorry.

A beat.

Mother   But where is she?

Daughter   Next door – a sleepover.

Mother   Isn't she a bit young?

Daughter   No. She asked to. She loves her, they're great friends. And I'm right here if anything goes wrong. She knows that.

Mother   Well.

A beat.

Daughter   And you know what I'm realising. I need time and space. To be me again. Sometimes. Sometimes I have to put myself first. Remember I have a name that isn't Mummy. That's allowed isn't it? You must feel that too. Feel you're more than just a mother. A grandmother.

No answer.

You're pale.

Mother   Well. I did get a shock. Silly really.

Daughter   I'm sorry you were upset.

Mother   But at least now I know you'll not go.

Daughter   What?

Mother   Your reaction on the phone – you think he's alive too, whatever you say. So you need to wait for him. Here.

Daughter   No. I owe him nothing. And as I tried to explain to you money is difficult.

Mother   If I had any I'd /

Daughter   It's not your responsibility – and I'm not asking. I'm just trying to explain to you why I think we probably will need to move. Eventually.

Mother   If he doesn't come back.

Daughter   But I promise we will always have space for you to come and stay – whenever you want. Ok? Don't worry.

A beat.

Now why don't you stay for dinner? I'm going to order pizza and watch telly.

Mother   No. No I just came to check on her – but if she's not here then I can't can I?

Daughter   No – not tonight. But you're doing bedtime tomorrow remember? I'll be back late from work.

Scene Ten

The kitchen. Evening. The **Mother** *has just put the child to bed. She comes into the kitchen with a holdall that is full. She puts it down and sits at the table with a pen and paper. She is trying to compose a note. She tries several times but abandons her attempts and ends up throwing the note in the bin.*

Pause.

She thinks.

She fixes the tea towels.

She resolves.

She puts on her coat.

She takes a deep breath.

She goes out into the hall and we hear her feet on the stairs.

Pause.

Now we hear her feet slowly coming downstairs.

She enters the kitchen. She is carrying the sleeping child in a blanket over her shoulder. She opens the back door and grabs the holdall.

She goes out and shuts the door behind her.

The sound of car doors opening and closing.

The sound of an engine starting and a car driving off.

Silence.

Long pause.

Keys in the door. **Daughter** *enters. She is going quietly. Gingerly. She sees the kitchen is empty and enters in a more relaxed way.*

She takes off her coat and pours herself a glass of wine, looking in the fridge considering what to cook. She looks at the clock. She decides to check on her child and the **Mother** *so heads upstairs.*

We hear her feet on the stairs.

Pause – more feet.

Pause.

Feet rushing down stairs and the **Daughter** *bursts into the kitchen. She is frantic. Unsure. She picks up the phone, then puts it down. Paces a mite more.*

Daughter   What the fuck –?

She picks up the phone, then puts it down. Paces a mite more.

THINK!

She looks at the tea towels. Suddenly she realises what has happened . . . she knows who has her child.

Fucking . . .

She goes to the counter and picks up a paring knife from the block.

I'll kill her . . . Fucking . . . Fucking . . .

She stops herself and stops her pacing and tries to breathe. She goes to the phone and breathes. She dials a number. She is holding the knife all the while.

Listen. I know what you've done. Bring her back and I'll tell you. Everything. About him. Why he left. You'll see him again. But you have to bring her back. First. Now. I'm waiting.

She puts down the phone. She is still holding the knife.

She is drained. She flops into a chair at the kitchen table. She faces the audience. Her hands are on her lap under the table.

Long pause. Her breathing is ragged.

She's mine. My girl. Cut from me.

She's mine My girl Cut from me.

She's mineMy girlCut from me

She'smineMygirlCut from me

She'smineMygirlCutfromme

minemygirlcutfromme

She's mine.

My girl.

Cut from me.

She lifts up her hands from her lap and they are covered in blood.

Blood. Am I. Dying. Again?

She passes out on the table. Blackout.

Scene Eleven

The kitchen. Evening. The **Mother** *is tidying. Suddenly she stops and goes to the back door and opens it. The* **Daughter** *is stood there, keys in her hand.*

Daughter   How did you know?

Mother   I was expecting you. And. Well! You're on time. Nice change.

Daughter   I told work. I have to leave on time now.

Mother   Well done.

A beat.

You look good. Bright. Would you like a cup of tea?

Daughter   No. Thanks. I was hoping to read her a story.

Mother   Ah. You've just missed her.

Daughter   But it's only /

Mother   Sparko.

Daughter   It's not even 7. She's normally only in the bath now.

Mother   She was tired.

Daughter   But it's early.

Mother   She goes to bed earlier. Now.

A beat.

Give me the keys.

Daughter   They're mine.

Mother   You need to give them to me.

They stare at one another. The **Daughter** *is furious. But she is also in a weak position. After a moment she gives in and hands over the keys. The* **Mother** *takes them without even acknowledging that they have been handed over.*

Mother   You know how she gets just before bed. Screamy. She goes from being quiet and drowsy to running around and screaming. Madly. Like a mad thing. Piercing. Through you. Well I realised that that was tiredness. Wasn't it? Of course. She's normally such a good girl. And if she goes to bed a bit earlier, well that's better. For everyone.

Daughter   But then she wakes up at /

Mother   I've always been an early riser myself.

A beat.

Daughter   Well. I might go and look at her then. She's always so angelic when she's asleep.

Mother   Wait a while. I don't want her disturbed.

Daughter   I wouldn't disturb /

Mother   Take off your coat. If you're staying a bit.

The **Daughter** *thinks for a moment then takes off her coat. And puts it on the back of a chair. The* **Mother** *moves it to a hook by the door.*

Now the coat is off we see there are bandages on the **Daughter**'s *wrists.*

Mother   Have a drink.

Daughter   Do you have any wine?

Mother   Is that a good idea – with the tablets?

Daughter   I'm fine.

A beat.

I bought her – a cuddly.

She takes a soft toy from her handbag.

Mother   She'll like that. I'll give it to her.

Daughter   I'll slip it under her arm when I go up – that way she'll have a nice surprise in the morning.

A beat.

Mother   Is there a knack with the airing cupboard?

Daughter   The door?

Mother   Yes. I think it's shut and then it pops open again.

Daughter   Oh – you have to press the button on the latch as you push it in. It's a bit fiddly. I can show you /

Mother   No I'll work it out.

Daughter   He was meant to fix it.

Mother   That wasn't his job.

A beat.

Daughter   I miss her

Mother   May I see the toy?

The **Daughter** *doesn't want her to touch it but again is in the weaker position so reluctantly hands it over. The* **Mother** *appraises it; it's soft and cuddly.*

Mother   Sweet. I'll give it to her.

Daughter   But I wanted to surprise –

Mother   Might make her feel strange. Or sad, that you were here and she missed you. I'll tell her it's from you. Don't worry. It'll be easier coming from me.

Daughter   But I wanted to see her reaction. Her little face when I gave it to her. The joy.

Mother   Well, you can't. Gifts are about the receiver not the giver.

Daughter   But I wanted –

Mother   It's not about you. She's not here for your pleasure. She doesn't exist for your enjoyment – whenever it suits you. That's not how this works.

The **Daughter** *looks like she might explode. But again she knows she can't.*

Pause.

Mother   Give it a minute and you can go and have a look at her.

Daughter   I miss her so much. I miss my house.

Mother   It wasn't up to me. The court. If you want me to take her elsewhere /

Daughter   No – I want her in her own home. What have you told her about me?

Mother   That you've not been well.

Daughter   Oh.

Mother   It's the truth. She asked if you were in heaven like her dad.

Daughter   Oh!

Mother   I've had trouble persuading her he's not dead.

Daughter   Better dead than abandoned her. I'm going up.

Mother   Sit back down. He didn't abandon us – it was you. Your behaviour. (*Stops herself.*) I don't want to get into this again. But he was always a very sensitive child. And he is a sensitive man.

Daughter   We're all sensitive.

Mother   You never told me what happened to him. In your message you said you know what happened.

Daughter   We fought – he left.

Mother   That's all? What did you do? Say?

Daughter   He walked away. From all of us. You too. It wasn't my fault. Blame him. Not me.

Mother   Men are different. They have a role – we have a role. You had a job. And you failed.

Daughter   And now I'm being punished, is that it?

Mother   As far as I can tell you are only punishing yourself. You need to go and get on with your life.

Daughter   My life? I can't.

She's mine. My girl. Mine. Cut from me. And once she was there. It was as though. He had never been. Born in blood. It's so normal.

Every day. He said. I agreed. Pretended. But it's not. Normal. It's
dying. It's putting your head in the jaws of death. All that blood.
Shit. Vomit. Vile. Hot. Heavy. And he didn't respect me for it. Said
it was like watching an animal. My face. That it twisted. Wasn't
mine. My hole – like the entrance to hell. He could never look at
me the same again. Afterwards. And I hated him. For that. For
changing me. And she was magnetised. To me. When she cried out
it caused me physical. Actual. Pain. Burning. In my breasts.
Between my legs. He wanted to get back to normal but there was
no. He wanted to get back between my legs. Normal. But after
what he'd seen. It wasn't the same. And he didn't like her. Said she
was all me. No him. And I didn't like him. Didn't want him. But I
did. Of course he decided to go. But the fight. Came first. I found
the pictures. He looked at. Piles of them. Legs. Flesh. Hands.
Mouths. I got dizzy. Got sick. Looking. Red. Lips. Mouths. Holes.
So I cut them. Up. Into pieces. Shredded. Tore. The legs. Flesh.
Hands. Mouths. They were everywhere. Couldn't escape. He
couldn't escape. Normal he said. They didn't look. Normal. Those
legs. Flesh. Hands. Mouths. So many mouths and holes and
tongues and flesh you couldn't tell where one person stopped and
the next started. I was. Disturbed. Normal he said. Yes but not
normal for us. For you. You have a daughter. Those women. Girls.
Not. Normal. And I have my needs. You don't give me what I
need. I should take what I need. You're an animal after all. Breath
in my face. I saw her come out of you and you are just an animal.
We are all just animals. You're disgusting. Look at your face.
You're an animal. Smell. Different. Of blood. Death. Taste. Putrid.
Decomposing. Animal. Who are you? This isn't you. Where did
you go? Where? Here. I'm here. It's still me. I'm real. Let's see if
I'm real. If you're real. Blade sharp. Clean. Metal. The blood.
Rising. In my head. See it. In my eyes. Red. His face. Blank.
Scared? Then gone. Disappeared. His face. Gone. Did that happen?
Did that really just happen? This isn't real life. It can't be. I'm
asleep. I'm just asleep. dreaming now. This isn't happening. Isn't
real. It can't be . . . She's upstairs asleep. Because she's my girl . . .
mine . . .

The child begins to cry loudly shouting, 'Mummy! Mummy!'

Both women get up, go to the door and put their hands on the handle. They look at each other. The **Mother** *pushes the* **Daughter** *out of the way and stands with her back to the door.*

Daughter   She wants me.

Mother   No she doesn't.

Daughter   I'm her mother.

Mother   Not anymore.

The crying and shouting get louder – almost hysterical. The **Daughter** *puts her hands over her ears.*

Daughter   I need to go to her. I can't bear it.

She tries to get past – the **Mother** *resists her.*

Mother   Crying won't kill her.

Daughter   Let me go to her . . .

She tries to pass again and fails.

You go – go to her. PLEASE!

Mother   If you want me to go to her I will.

She exits. We hear her go upstairs, then we hear her shhing the child. The **Daughter** *is upset, pacing, but as the child calms so does she.*

But then she hears the **Mother** *speak to the child.*

Mother   It's ok – I'm here – Mummy's here.

At this the **Daughter** *goes to the knife rack, picks up a large knife and heads out of the room, upstairs.*

Blackout.